WHY ARE ANIMALS RED?

Melissa Stewart

Series Literacy Consultant:
Allan A. De Fina, PhD
Dean, College of Education/Professor of Literacy
Education, New Jersey City University
Past President of the New Jersey Reading Association

Series Science Consultant:
Helen Hess, PhD
Professor of Biology
College of the Atlantic
Bar Harbor, Maine

Contents

Words to Know 3

A Rainbow of Animals 4

Red Animals Near You 6

Scarlet Ibis 8

Bald Uakari 10

Northern Cardinal 12

Great Frigate Bird 15

Coral Snake 17

Morpho Caterpillars 19

White-tipped Soldierfish 20

Radiant Sea Urchins 22

Pacific Giant Octopus 25

Guessing Game 26

Where Do These Red Animals Live? 28

Learn More:
Books 30
Web Sites 31

Index 32

Words to Know

attract (uh TRAKT)—To make interested; to get the attention of.

blend in—To match; to look the same as.

poison (POY zun)—A material that makes an animal sick. Sometimes the animal gets so sick that it dies.

predator (PREH duh tur)—An animal that hunts and kills other animals for food.

survive (sur VYV)—To stay alive.

northern
cardinal

yellow boxfish

A Rainbow of Animals

panther chameleon

poison dart
frog

Go outside and look around. How many kinds of animals do you see? Snakes and birds are animals. So are spiders and insects. Animals come in all sizes and shapes. And they come in all the colors of the rainbow.

leaf-mimic katydid

lesser purple
emperor butterfly

Red Animals Near You

Can you think of some red animals that live near you? Some snakes are red. So are some birds and insects.

Red animals live in other parts of the world, too. Let's take a look at some of them.

Scarlet Ibis

This bird is gray and white when it hatches from its egg. The chick eats lots of red crabs. This food changes the color of its feathers. By the time the bird is full grown, its body is bright red.

Bald Uakari

What do female uakaris (wah KAH rees) look for in a mate? A very red face. It means the male monkey is healthy, and he will make a good father.

Northern Cardinal

This male's bright colors send the same kind of message. They tell females he is strong and healthy. He will do a good job protecting the nest. And he will find lots of food for their chicks.

Great Frigate Bird

This bird's feathers are not red. But he still knows how to **attract** a female. He pumps air into a red pouch on his throat. Females can see it from far away.

Coral Snake

This snake's red rings send out a different message. They say, "Stay away!" If a **predator** gets too close, the snake will give it a painful bite full of **poison**.

Morpho Caterpillars

These caterpillars do not need to hide. They stay in a group instead. That makes them look like one large red creature. Most hungry birds will not go near them.

White-tipped Soldierfish

On land, red animals are easy to see. But at night in the ocean, red creatures are hard to spot. These red fish **blend in** with their watery world. That helps them hide from larger fish and other enemies.

Radiant Sea Urchins

Even on bright sunny days, these ocean animals do not have to hide. Their long red spines give a painful sting. It is enough to keep most predators away.

Pacific Giant Octopus

What does this octopus do when it spots an enemy? It changes its skin color to blend in with the rocks nearby.

Guessing Game

Being red helps many kinds of animals **survive** in the world. It helps some animals send a message to mates or predators. It helps other animals hide from their enemies. How do you think being red helps the animals in these photos?

strawberry poison dart frogs

(See answers on page 32.)

mandrill

Where Do These Red

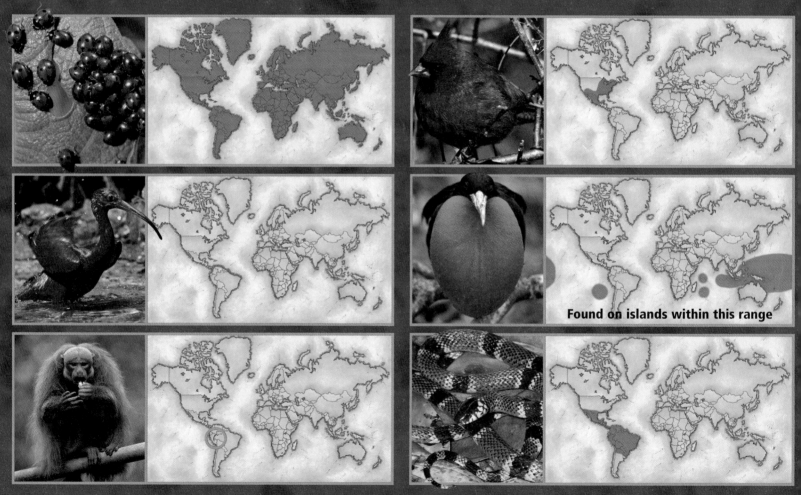

Found on islands within this range

Animals Live?

KEY:
The orange areas on each map below show where that animal lives.

Learn More

Books

Jenkins, Steve. *Living Color*. Boston: Houghton Mifflin, 2007.

Kalman, Bobbie, and John Crossingham. *Camouflage: Changing to Hide*. New York: Crabtree Publishing, 2005.

Stockland, Patricia. *Red Eyes or Blue Feathers: A Book About Animal Colors*. Minneapolis: Picture Window Books, 2005.

Whitehouse, Patricia. *Colors We Eat: Red Foods*. Chicago: Heinemann, 2004.

Learn More

Web Sites

Animal Colors
   http://www.highlightskids.com/Science/Stories/SS1000_
      animalColors.asp

Beasts Playground: Camouflage Game
   http://www.abc.net.au/beasts/playground/camouflage.htm

How Animal Camouflage Works
   http://science.howstuffworks.com/animal-camouflage1.htm

Index

A attract, 15

C changing color, 25
        chick, 8, 12

E egg, 8
        enemies, 20, 26

F face, 10
        father, 10
        feathers, 8, 15

H hatch, 8
        healthy, 10, 12
        hide, 19, 20, 22, 26

M mate, 10, 15, 26

N nest, 12

P poison, 17
        pouch, 15
        predator, 17, 22, 26

R rings, 17

S spines, 22
        sting, 22
        survive, 26

T throat, 15

Enslow Elementary, an imprint of Enslow Publishers, Inc.

Enslow Elementary ® is a registered trademark of Enslow Publishers, Inc.

Copyright © 2009 by Melissa Stewart

Library of Congress Cataloging-in-Publication Data

Stewart, Melissa.
    Why are animals red? / Melissa Stewart.
       p. cm. — (Rainbow of animals)
    Includes bibliographical references.
    Summary: "Uses examples of animals in the wild to explain why some animals are red"—Provided by publisher.
    ISBN 978-0-7660-3249-1
    1. Animals—Color—Juvenile literature. 2. Red—Juvenile literature. I. Title.
    QL767.S749 2009
    591.47'2—dc22   2008011472

ISBN-10: 0-7660-3249-3

Printed in the United States of America
042010 Lake Book Manufacturing, Inc., Melrose Park, IL

10 9 8 7 6 5 4 3 2

To Our Readers: We have done our best to make sure all Internet Addresses in this book were active and appropriate when we went to press. However, the author and the publisher have no control over and assume no liability for the material available on those Internet sites or on other Web sites they may link to. Any comments or suggestions can be sent by e-mail to comments@enslow.com or to the address on the back cover.

Interior: Minden Pictures: © Barry Mansell/npl, p. 5 (frog); © Chris Newbert, p. 4 (boxfish); © Claus Meyer, pp. 10–11, 28 (uakari); © Cyril Ruoso/TH Editorial, pp. 27, 29 (mandrill); © Frans Lanting, p. 5 (katydid); © Fred Bavendam, pp. 1 (top right), 20–21, 24–25, 29 (fish, octopus); © Georgette Douwma/npl, pp. 1 (bottom left), 22–23, 29 (urchins); © Hans Cristoph Kappel/npl, p. 5 (butterfly); © Konrad Wothe, pp. 1 (bottom right), 6–7, 28 (ladybugs); © Michael & Patricia Fogden, pp. 16–17, 28 (coral snake); © Mitsuhiko Imamori, pp. 3, 26, 29 (dart frogs); © Pete Oxford, p. 4 (chameleon); © Rod Williams/npl, pp. 1 (top left), 8–9, 28 (ibis); © Tom Vezo, pp. 4 (cardinal), 12–13, 28 (cardinal); © Tui De Roy, pp. 14–15, 28 (frigate bird).

© Luiz Claudio Marigo/naturepl.com, pp. 18–19, 29 (caterpillars).

Cover: Minden Pictures: (clockwise from top left): © Rod Williams; © Fred Bavendam; © Konrad Wothe; © Georgette Douwma/npl.

Illustration Credits: © 1999, Artville, LLC, pp. 28–29 (maps).

Note to Parents and Teachers: The *Rainbow of Animals* series supports the National Science Education Standards for K–4 science. The Words to Know section introduces subject-specific vocabulary words, including pronunciation and definitions. Early readers may need help with these new words.

Answers to the Guessing Game:

The bright skin of poison dart frogs warn enemies to stay away. The skin is full of poison.

Mandrills live in thick, dark forests. How do these monkeys find one another? They look for the bright red noses of their friends and family.

Enslow Elementary
an imprint of
Enslow Publishers, Inc.

40 Industrial Road
Box 398
Berkeley Heights, NJ 07922
USA

http://www.enslow.com